ARCHANGELOLOGY URIEL PEACE

IF YOU CALL THEM THEY WILL COME

KIM CALDWELL

Archangelology LLC

A Division of Archangelology LLC

https://archangelology.com

Copyright © 2017 by Kim Caldwell

All rights reserved.

No part of this book may be reproduced in any form or by any electronic or mechanical means, including information storage and retrieval systems, without written permission from the author, except for the use of brief quotations in a book review.

This publication is designed to provide competent and reliable information regarding the subject matter covered. However, it is sold with the understanding that the author and publisher are not engaged in rendering medical and healthcare or any advice. Archangelology LLC, Together Publishing and all offerings are for entertainment purpose only. If you need medical, financial or any kind of help please consult a qualified professional.

Introduction Editing and enhancement Rachel Caldwell

Book Editing Grammarly

ISBN: 978-1-947284-39-5

Book Cover Picture Nicola Zalewski

Cover design Kim Caldwell

❦ Created with Vellum

1
ABOUT THE SERIES

"Logic will get you from point A to B. Imagination will take you everywhere."--Einstein

This Archangelology book and the entire series aim to lift the reader one step at a time. You may read this piece anytime you desire Upliftment and want to feel good now, never underestimate the power of feeling good for creating more of what you want.

Choose this or any of the other Archangelology Books or Matching Audios to read or listen to for at least 44 nights and raise your vibration consistently for an Uplifted Feeling and Life.

This piece is one of a series of Angelic Upgrade books that fill you with Divine Angelic codes. Angelic laws are based on love and light and thus, operate for free-will, so we must call and ask the Archangels for help.

When working with your book relax, take deep breaths and ground to Mother Earth. Focus on Intentions for whatever it is your heart desires that are for the highest good of all involved. Intentions for these energies that we can not see but feel when we are ready. There are those that believe The Archangels are the Ones that make Law of Attraction Work.

This series of books take on a life of its own as the Archangels move and play from book to book, creating a Delicious Alchemy. Each book becomes an instrument in this Celestial Symphony for a more fulfilling life. Many of the Archangel books also carry and infuse the Violet Flame and Divine Connection to Mother Earth for a transformational experience.

Each book has a matching meditation audio available for your listening pleasure at https://archangelology.com. Please visit our site for your gifts. The book and the audio have similar wording, yet according to the Angels, they Upgrade us differently. Each medium has a unique experience, energetically Upgrading us in distinct ways. Each time you read or hear an Archangel Upgrade, a new dimension is added or adjusted for your benefit.

Become interactive with your book; when inspired, read the words aloud, and let them roll over you, feeling the love and magic that the Angels radiate. When inspired create your own rituals; there is no right or wrong way. As you play with the rock stars of the Celestial realm, you can expect your life to become more heavenly, more peaceful.

You may Notice Many Words are Uniquely Capitalized throughout this series; this is yet another way the Angels infuse us. When you see this try to feel that word or phrase; sensing the depth of its Intensity of Pure Divine Light throughout your Being.

The Archangel Energy is neither male

nor female. This gender fluidity is made clear in this series by the use of the word they or he/she speak to convey a non-gender energy that shifts roles to uplift and nurture you. The upgrades happen in Divine Time, and there is no schedule. There is no competition. There is no rush. Wherever you are in the process is perfect.

A word about the length of this book. "Less is more." This Series of books is the result of decades of study in the art of Law of Attraction, Angelic knowing and energy healing, condensed here for you in a format that will shift and benefit the reader. If you found your way here, you can expect miracles. As Einstein said, "There are only two ways to live your life. One is as though nothing is a miracle. The other is as though everything is a miracle." The matching audio to this book is 44 minutes, so working with that is always an option.

Both Neville Goddard and Albert Einstein stated that our imagination is the creative force. Goddard went so far as to imply that our imagination is the God/dess Energy. I mention this to you because as you read these words with much more than your eyes, let your imagination run wild with vivid pictures of the love the magical Archangels have for you and of your adventures together. Enjoy.

2

ABOUT ARCHANGEL URIEL

If you Desire more peace and protection in your life, call Archangel Uriel. Uriel fills every part of your life with Peace when you call her/him. Take a walk with her/him in a gorgeous light field where Divine Love and Peace infuse every cell of your mind, body, and spirit. Uriel teaches you to see everyone and everything as white light and allow it to all flow together and become peaceful Oneness. Archangel Uriel helps your Earth Angel Wings come in so you may soar to new heights in your life. These Celestial Wings also remind you that time is just an illusion and teach you how to time travel with the Archangels. Enjoy an exercise to bring more love in any relationship you like, while working on remembering how truly worthy you are. Uriel shines such sweet unconditional love upon you that you feel amazing and perfect. See yourself in a new light as Archangel Uriel shines deep sweet peace on you and your life. Allow this feeling of peace to take over your life and Universe, remembering you too are an Earth Angel. As you remember your natural angelic abilities, float in deep space with Uriel as you enjoy delicious celestial infusions of love and light. Feel the love of Mother Earth as you connect to her for Deep Peace. Become heart centered with love and send this to any situation in your life that you would like to better. Send Angelic peace to any person with whom you would like to get along better.

Archangel Metatron makes a guest appearance to infuse our lives with delicious Sacred Geometry with Uriel's Peace magic. It is gorgeous Archangel Alchemy at its best for healing yourself and your relationships. Adapting these mindsets will help shift your consciousness and make you a magnet for confidence, peace, and prosperity in new refreshed ways. There is no right or wrong way to use this tool. All these Divinely Intelligent Angelic Upgrades happen with grace and ease at the individual's comfortable pace. The only thing I recommend you keep in the forefront of your practice is to ensure you are enjoying the process. Meet the Archangels in the Archangelology Book and Audio Series that is here to help you at this time. If you call on Uriel, she/he will come, just as all of the Archangels will come to your assistance when beckoned. Spending time with Archangels creates a heavenly life. For gifts from the Archangels visit https://archangelology.com.

3

ARCHANGEL URIEL PEACE

Archangelology. Uriel. Princess/Prince of Peace. Take a deep, healing breath now. And feel the brilliant Archangel Uriel standing before you. Gaze upon her/his whole gloriousness. The Angels want to let you know that their energy is neither male nor female. It is a blending of the best qualities of the female energies and the best qualities of the male energies. Along with the God/dess Force.

The Angels' energy is so beautiful. So pure. So bright. So blessed, so Divine. And Archangel Uriel is shining her/his Divine, peaceful light upon you now. Deep healing breath.

Just relax, as every cell of your body takes in Archangel Uriel's peaceful, emanating, loving waves of energy that consume you now and bring you to states of great bliss. Of great ecstasy. Of great knowing. What a Divine. Feel this. Perfect. Take it in. How deserving. Of all the love and all the light and all the blessings you are. You are so brilliant; you are magnificent. Archangel Uriel wants you to feel this deep radiating in your heart center.

Deep healing breath. Feel this now. Feel all the love. Feel all the peace, radiating to you, and breath it in deeply. Archangel Uriel has many, many gifts, as all the Angels do. One of his specialties is bringing peace into any situation, into any soul, into any being, into any world, in any dimension. There is no atom small enough, no place far enough, that Archangel cannot bring her/his Divine, sweet, healing, peaceful, loving energies.

Let it shimmer on you now. Yes, feel it, with all your heart, with all your soul, radiating, into you. Now, feel Archangel Uriel's white light shimmering through your body, filling you with peace, bringing you into this Divine Now Moment, into this perfect, joyous moment. Deep healing breath.

Feel streams of white light, moving into your third eye, your crown chakra, moving through your whole chakra system, lighting up your chakra system, invigorating you. Now you're going to feel white light going up, up from the ground, coming up through your base chakra, moving through all your chakras, all the way up, up, yes. Now I want you to see that beautiful white light, moving all the way up your spine, moving out of your head like a sprinkler, yes.

And watch as this beautiful light just keeps flowing up and cleaning and clearing. Yes, removing any blocks, filling you with deep, peaceful love. A deep healing breath. Feel this now. Feel the shimmers of white light, cleaning, clearing, healing. Yes, feel your whole body come alive with the sweet, divine energies of love, peace, and light. Take a deep, beautiful, healing breath as the Archangel Uriel helps you clear any fears, any heavy thoughts. Anything that takes you away from your peace is being gently drawn up and out and shimmering out of your head now, just shimmering over and up.

All the light is sparkling, and your mind is tingling with love and peace, and before you, stands the beautiful Archangel Uriel, watching with such a look of peace, with such a knowing of how Divine you are in every moment. And you continue to let this white light flow as you feel Archangel Uriel supporting you, loving you, being there with you, staying with you always. Uriel communicates with you now and lets you know they've always been there for you. And when you call, Uriel will fill you and your world with this beautiful peace. All you need do is ask.

If inspired, hold your hand up and take a deep breath and repeat after me now: "Archangel Uriel. I call on you now. I ask you for your Divine, Graceful Peace. I ask for your help in all aspects of my life. I ask you to shed peace in my mind, my body, my spirit. I ask you to shimmer my life with deep, sweet, Divine Peace." Deep breath.

Now, Archangel Uriel gazes upon you in

all her/his beauty, in all her/his gorgeousness, with a look that gives you such a feeling of contentment and belonging that it just melts all your defenses and you know you are so safe. Deep healing breath. Archangel Uriel puts out her/his hand. She/He wants to take us on a walk.

The night is still, the sky's a deep midnight blue, the white shimmering Stars Sparkle in the sky. You take a deep breath; you feel invigorated. She/He leads you to a beautiful meadow where you notice that all the tall, fresh smelling grass is white, light. It's stunningly beautiful. All the grass moves in the soft, gentle breeze. And there's this white light all around you, and you walk, and the peace emanating from this beautiful place, and the peace emanating from Archangel Uriel is filling every part of you. Your physical body, every cell, your mental body, your spiritual body, all your bodies, every part is being filled with love, light, peace, and ignited now. As you walk, the beautiful grass touches your legs and gently soothes and caresses you as you hold Uriel's hand. You walk together. Uriel is telepathically telling you now to practice with him/her, seeing things as white light. Letting you know that this brings beautiful peace into your life.

Uriel wants you to know that you can see all the beings, all the places, all the things around you when you're out in the world as pure, white light. Deep healing breath. She's/He's letting you know that when you do this, the more you do this, the easier it will become for you and the more you will feel the deep, delicious warmness that is the reality and the more you will know that any separateness that we have imagined is an illusion.

You may take Archangel Uriel and this tool with you to any room, to any place, and you may start to see all the beings around you, all the objects around you shimmer and turn into beautiful, healing white light. Feel it, feel the power of this now. Now, Uriel, has you stand to face her/him. And she/he puts up her/his finger, and she/he puts it right on your third eye, when Archangel Uriel does this, a tube encompasses you and you become bright, shimmering, brilliant white light. Feel it now. Deep healing breath. Yes. Feel yourself shimmering. Feel the pure, beautiful white light enveloping you—yes, feel how you merge with everything around you: the grass, the beautiful white, light grass.

Now, Uriel has a special treat for you. Uriel turns to pure, white shimmering light right before you. Yes, and you smile, and you watch in awe and amazement as she/he moves her/his energy closer to yours, as you and Uriel become One beautiful tube of shimmering white, healing, Divine, Light. Feel this now. Ahhh. Take a deep breath. And just sigh into the deliciousness of this experience with Archangel Uriel, the beautiful Princess/Prince of peace.

Feel every cell in your body tingle, shimmer, and release anything that no longer serves you. Yes. With sweet white light, feel the sounds like waves of love and peace flowing through your body. And now, as your standing there with the beautiful Archangel Uriel, your personal friend and guide, who adores you beyond anything you ever imagined.

Archangel Uriel has another surprise for

you, and you smile because you know it's something you're going to love so much. Archangel Uriel touches your heart with her divine finger, and your heart chakra starts to radiate such love, and Uriel reminds you, this is what you always intended, to think with your heart, to love with your heart, to live with your heart.

You thank your intelligence and mind for the job they've done, and you allow Archangel Uriel to anchor you now in the beautiful heart-centered thinking that is your divine birthright. Uriel reminds you that as you start to be heart-centered, your life will become more and more magnificent.

Divinity on new levels will appear. Beautiful beings will appear. Yes, your heart radiates; I can see a beautiful sacred geometry, a shimmering light heart, right there at your heart center, healing, translucent, opalescent, beyond beauty, beyond divinity, beyond words. How safe and peaceful you are at this moment. Deep healing breath.

Oh, yes. Thank you, thank you, Archangel Uriel, for this beautiful gift that you bestow upon us when we ask ...if inspired, hold your hand up and ask with me now, 'Archangel Uriel, keep me heart-centered in my life. Remind me, guide me, help me to stay in this beautiful place more and more, and let me know that it's okay when I fall away from it, that you'll always be waiting, and you'll always guide me back to this magical, beautiful place that we have created together'. Deep healing breath.

Now, as you stand in your beautiful tube, infused together with Archangel Uriel and such divine blessed peace that you can't imagine how things could get better, Archangel Uriel reminds you that he has another blessed gift for you that you've been waiting for ... that you knew you would get one day, yes. Archangel Uriel with all his grace and divinity touches your third eye, and as he does, you feel a warm, tingling, divine feeling at your back as your beautiful, light, etheric Angel Wings start to appear. Yes. Deep healing breath.

Your wings are in full force now. They are magnificent; they shimmer with light, you can feel them, they're there ... you are so deserving of your beautiful, Archangel etheric wings. Deep healing breath. Feel them, feel your wings. Now, Archangel Uriel imparts to you the knowing that you may activate your wings at any moment you choose. You may activate your wings to bring more love and light into your Divine Soul, into your being, into your mind, into your heart, into the cells of your body. If you need more peace, if you need better being, you may simply close your eyes for a second and picture your wings, your healing, clearing, magnificent, energetically sparkling, all amazing, all powerful, all doing Angel Wings, and they are there for you at any moment.

No one knows but you. It is your special secret with Archangel Uriel. She/He lets you know to keep this to yourself, to keep your magic to yourself, to keep it strong. No one but you and your Archangel need to know, and you may activate your wings at any moment to send shimmering Angelic Love to anyone you see who needs it at the moment. You are an Earth Angel. You are an Earth Ambassador, here from heaven's most celestial realms.

There's another ability that our Angel

Wings give us: our ability to Time Travel into other dimensions. Time is just an illusion; time is not real; there is no aging; our bodies are eternal and youthful as long as we believe this to be so. Deep healing breath. Take a moment with Uriel now to visualize yourself in the tube of white healing light, see your wings in any capacity that you like. Allow them just to be shown to you, and see yourself standing there, completely, completely naked with your wings.

It's just you, it's just Uriel, showing such sweet unconditional love upon you that you can feel nothing but amazing. And feel how beautiful and perfect Uriel sees you. Feel that unconditional love just radiating. See your skin glowing. See your eyes sparkling. See Archangel Uriel smiling upon you with such pride, such joy. See the peace radiating and relaxing through your shoulders. Yes. Feel your body adjust, see that you feel comfortable and perfect at the moment, in your skin.

Yes, the peace, the peace radiates throughout you, with you, through all time and being, through all time and space, through all dimensions, you are sending peace. Now, come back to your glory and to whatever beautiful, Divine, comfortable clothing you like to adorn yourself with as an Angelic Being.

Archangel Uriel wants to show you something. Take a deep healing breath. Archangel Uriel is showing you a beautiful, beautiful, brilliant, panoramic ... screen. You and she are floating in deep space. Now take a deep breath and be grounded while you float; you can see yourself and Archangel Uriel floating outside the earth. Deep healing breath.

The sky is so clear and soft, the celestial sounds of the angels all around you. This is how an angel feels, your angel wings are active, barely fluttering unless you want them to flutter more. Angel wings don't take a lot of effort. It's like breathing; it's something you, as an earth angel, do naturally. You're coming into your natural, beautiful, magical, angel, angelic abilities.

Now, you visualize yourself and the gorgeous Archangel Uriel floating over the earth, and you see the earth glowing in beautiful, divine energy. And then, you feel all the love of the divine Mother Earth, our beautiful, beautiful Gaia. Feel this with Archangel Uriel now; feel it. Feel the love of Mother Earth. Feel that she supplies us, she gives, and she gives. Connect, connect with that earth love, with that earth energy. Yes, there you are. Deep healing breath.

Yes, Uriel is so proud. Uriel is shining such deep, sweet, divine love onto ... our glorious Mother Earth. Yes, yes, yes. Become so heart-centered with the love that you're feeling. As you do this, anytime you do this; Archangel Uriel wants you to know that you can send peace to any situation that you need. That by connecting to the Goddess that is Mother Earth, to the stream of life that nurtures and supplies, we can magically send love and light to any situation in our life that we need help with. To any person in our life that we would like more peace and love with.

See their face now. See their face, anyone that you would love to get along better with, hold that person's face and watch as all the shimmering rays of white light fill that beautiful, benevolent being. Now. Yes. Hold, that. And let that white light fill their soul. See that being now as pure, radiating white light

... see it, see their Divinity, hold it. You've got it. You're magic. You always suspected you were. Deep healing breath.

Now, there's a second step to this. But you'll only do it when you're ready. You see them as white light too, and you merge with that being, and you let it just be, just relax. And you let the beautiful, sacred geometry move throughout the whole situation with that person and heal, clear, and cleanse the energies. We have a visit, from Archangel Metatron. Archangel Metatron has her/his book and audio; Archangel Metatron is infusing white light with Archangel Uriel ... we have some Angel Alchemy going on here.

It is Divine. Feel how your body is tingling. Deep breath. The sacred geometry, all the shapes, all the beautiful, beautiful shapes, working on this situation with this person that you'd like to get along better with. Yes, the healing, feel it as the shapes move around and as Archangel Metatron stands in his/her golden tube of light beside you. And Archangel Uriel stands on the other side in her/his beautiful, white tube of light along with you and your benevolent friend or loved one. They may be alive; they may have passed into the nonphysical. It doesn't matter, through all time, space, dimensions. This healing is happening now. Deep healing breath.

And just feel as the beautiful Archangel magic happens, and know that it is done. Deep healing breath. Archangel Uriel now takes you by the hand and telepathically lets you know how deeply and Divinely proud of you she/he is, how you are now a radiating being of white healing light anytime you so choose. Uriel takes your hand and walks you ... to an area where there's a beautiful soft twilight energy. And a beautiful, beautiful ... open, airy ... building of sorts, and it's part of nature. There's like a canopy above your head that shields you, it's sheer and you can still see the Stars and Moon above you.

Archangel Uriel takes you to the most beautiful, beautiful bed you've ever seen. The sheets are white; the pillows are so fluffy that when you lay your head on them, you melt into these Divine Pillows. The mattress is like nothing you've ever felt before; it's beyond Divine. And Archangel Uriel helps you into the bed now and telepathically lets you know that one of his best gifts to you, is sleep, is rest.

He reminds you that when you rest, you meet, with all your other Angels, with all your guides, with all of the Ascended Masters, with all of the beings of light. Repeat after me and say with me now, 'Archangel Uriel, please keep me safe when I sleep. Please keep me in the higher, lighter dimensions. Please stay with me. Be with me and help me have peaceful, peaceful Divine Sleep'. Deep healing breath.

You know it is done. Now, Uriel lets you know it's time to get ... super comfy in the bed. Take a deep healing breath. This bed is the most comfortable and beautiful space you've ever been in, and you know that the angels have created this just for you. This is your special, angelic, white-light bed that you can return to anytime. And when you lay in this bed, from the mattress will emanate waves of divine peace ... wellness ... joy ... abundance ... bliss ... creativity ... wisdom ... anything you can imagine.

Archangel Uriel reminds you to take a

deep breath and feel this. 'Your wish is my command.' Archangel Uriel reminds you to be patient. Yes, we'll add patience to that list of things that emanates from this bed. Release any desire to become attached to results. Just float and surrender now with the angels and know that divine intelligence is activated. Say with me now, 'I ask Archangel Uriel and all the archangels to calm my ego. I thank my ego for all it's done and let it calm down and relax. I ask that all my thinking, all my interactions, become heart-centered now. I ask that all my thinking be done with my beautiful, compassionate angel heart now that I step into my angel, earth angel role'. Deep healing breath.

Now, you get a little comfier, and Archangel Uriel fluffs your pillows for you because she loves you and loves to see you happy and feel comfy and peaceful. There is nothing that the angels love more than to see you happy and smiling and relaxed. As you lay back, Archangel Uriel helps you feel peaceful by placing her hand right over your heart chakra. Now, Uriel lets you know that any place on your body that needs a little extra love, that needs a little healing, you may simply let Archangel Uriel know where that area is and she will move her angelic, divine hand to that area and flood that area with pure light.

As Archangel Uriel floods this area, for now, it's happening. Anything that no longer serves, any thoughts, any emotions, any implants, any cords, anything that doesn't need to be there is gently, with grace and ease, dissolved away with the beautiful, sparkling, white, peaceful light of Archangel Uriel. And you lay there smiling and understanding how magical this process is. And you take a deep healing breath and just let it happen, with no attachment, with not needing to know when you'll feel better, just knowing that, in its own divine time, it will happen, you will be at peace.

You will feel divine; you are divine, you are at peace. Deep healing breath. And you let Archangel Uriel work on you, feel you, with that healing, deep peace that brings on such well-being, that brings on such joy, that brings on such bliss. Yes, it's so beautiful. You are so divine. You are a gorgeous, gorgeous earth angel and all the archangels and Archangel Uriel love you more than you can imagine, and your imagination is expanding, you're cultivating your imagination. You're opening yourself to more and more love and light.

You are seen now. You see, you feel, how deeply, divinely, loved you are. Let that tingle throughout your whole body. Yes. You look into Archangel Uriel's eyes and he lets you know he is always here for you, he will always infuse you with peace, love, light, wellness. All you need do is ask. Take a deep healing breath. Archangel Uriel lets you know that together, you are anchoring this energy that is part of you now. It is part of your divine being. If inspired, say with me now, deep breath, 'I am an earth angel, I am divine, I am light, I am love, I am divine peace. I am what I am. Thank you, thank you, Archangel Uriel, Prince of Peace.'

4
ANGELIC HABITS

There is a saying that our habits make us who we are.

The habit of calling in our Angels creates more peace and poise. As we stop, take a deep breath and call our Angels, this is an opportunity to ground into the now moment and, if we are really on our game, also ground into our beautiful mother earth.

Calling our Angels takes practice and forethought it is a wonderful way to calm fear or anxiety. Acknowledging this Angelic Support allows us to see perceived "challenges" as opportunities. Reminding us that we are never alone and are supported by the

Celestial Masters, the Archangels, and much more.

Make reminders for yourself in convenient places where you will see them stop, breathe and call your Angels.

Do you have an event coming up? Call your Angels now and let them line things up smoothly for you. Allow the Divine Intelligence of the universe to help you.

Please be patient with yourself and with your Angels. Let attachment to outcome go, and as they say, "go with the flow."

Please remember that Angels are on Divine Time, so let go of when you think things "should happen" and allow yourself to relax. Play with this and have fun just like you did as a kid. You can do it and enjoy the process.

5

ANGELIC MANIFESTATION JOURNAL BONUS

Create more of the life you want with the Archangels as you explore and focus with your Angelic Journal. If you are ready, let's set intentions now to make your Archangel Michael Book a Manifestation tool. It is said that humans have so many thoughts going on in our heads at once that it is hard for Angels and Spirit Guides to hear what we want help with. This is one of the many reasons it is so powerful to get very clear on what we desire and write it out in a designated journal for our Archangels. This way, they can understand our needs better and help us with our dreams and goals in Divine Time.

It has been proven that when we write things down, more of what we desire comes to us. Goals get accomplished, and things flow with more ease. Adding the Amazing Archangels to your journaling just makes the results that much stronger. As we set intentions for what we want and take the time to focus and write it down in our journal, unseen forces move on our behalf. We are going to enlist the help of this Divine Knowing with our Archangel book in an interactive way and turn our book into a manifestation tool. We are also going to play with our books like children and have some fun. Children are powerful creators, and we will take on some of their great habits for their creative value.

Focus and underline ideas you resonate with in your book and become immersed in Upliftment. There is a deeper connection as we become interactive with our Archangel books. We may get colored pens and underline areas of our book that feel important or special to us. We may want to draw pictures of desired blessings or anything that makes us feel good. We may want to mark different areas of our book with hearts, stars, or Angel wings. Get sticky tab notes, a personal favorite, and stick them to your favorite pages you want to return to often. In your journal section, place a sticky tab on an area you want to let the Angels know to help you write in and as a personal reminder. Let your Angelic interaction and intuition guide you with what feels best. Neville Goddard and Albert Einstein both explained that our imagination is a creative force and can bring great blessings to our lives. We will bring our imagination fully into our process now. You may want to add stickers to enhance pages. Place a beautiful angel or magic looking card in your book as a bookmark. Get creative and give your book some personal character. Putting clover or flowers in your book to press and dry, adds some powerful nature magic to your process. Roses are a great choice as they have the highest vibration of any flower. You may give lovely flowers as an offering to your Archangels as well. Giving back is always a beneficial activity.

    Everyone has magical abilities. Some of

us know this, and some do not. My point is all these ideas are simple and will work for anyone who puts forth an effort and has the faith to relax and let go so the angels may do their work. Of course, anything we put out comes back to us, so we want to always include "for the highest good" in all requests.

In all my studies of magical herbs, cinnamon is found in many different traditions for enhancement of all things wanted and removing things not wanted. You may want to rub a dab of cinnamon mixed with a touch of olive oil on your journal in an intentional shape such as a heart for more love or the infinity symbol for more abundance. Then say to yourself, "I anoint my journal with success and happiness with the help of the Archangels." Anointment has been practiced for eons with much luck and advancement. Basil and Sage could just as easily be utilized. Anything that feels magical and speaks to you in your spice cabinet most likely has wonderful magical properties. Use these gifts of nature with intention and focus for a more joyous life. The idea is to create a magnet for all you desire that is for your highest good with your Archangel Journal.

You may want to underline ideas in colors that mean something to you. The sky is the limit, get creative and juicy with your book, knowing that amazing things are being created.

Next, we have dedicated pages that are waiting for you to fill them with your heart's desires that Michael will help you achieve as long as they are for the highest good. You may write anything you want in your Archangel Journal. There is no right or wrong way to do this. You may ask the Archangels to help you release things from your life, share your hopes and dreams, or ask questions. I love to ask my angels questions and patiently wait to know they will lead me to the answer in Divine Time. Be open and honest with your journaling and the Archangels understanding that the only ones who need to see your Angel Journal are you and your Angels. Keeping your wishes to yourself is very powerful for manifesting as well.

We have created categories for you, and of course, there will Be freestyle areas, so play with this and have fun. After you play with your journal, you may put it away in a sacred space knowing all is in Divine Order. Remember, magic works just in its own time and asking where the results are will only block things, so relax, have faith, and patience. You may come back to read your Archangel book and add more to it at any time. Know that unseen beneficial forces are moving to help you now and forevermore. Play with and collect other Archangelology books and audios, remembering, "If you call them, they will come." Check out the Archangelology Archangel Journaling Book for more ideas on taking your Journaling Process to the next "celestial" level. The Archangels have tied this whole series Together for us in such a Divinely Intelligent way. Spend time in nature with your book, filling it with love, imagination, and Angelic magic for exponential results. You are a powerful creator and loved by all that is.

Write on the blank areas of your book

and on the lined journal areas. Think outside of the box and let your kid like creative energies flow. Have fun, and add your own flair.

Please enjoy the process and expect wonderful things.

6
PEACE WITH ARCHANGEL URIEL

Feel as you relax into Archangel Uriels immense calming wings. Allow heavenly sprinkles of soft blue light to shimmer and soothe all around you. Listen as Archangel Uriel gently reminds you to connect to your higher self for more calm and wisdom. Journal all the beautiful things you hear and feel.

7
RELAXING WITH ARCHANGEL URIEL

Get super comfy and visualize Archangel Uriel with you. Feel Archangel Uriel encouraging you to take slow, deep breaths and relax.

Imagine a shimmering blue ball of light in front of you filled with peace and tranquility. Think about and list anything you would love to let go of, and listen for Archangel Uriel's guidance. Allow your self-love to flow all over your Journal. Allow your freedom and "peace" of Mind. Shimmer your life with Calm.

8

CALM MIND WITH ARCHANGEL URIEL

Call Archangel Uriel and ask for their assistance in achieving a calm mind more often. Archangel Uriel is a master at the art of peaceful protection. Call on them to protect your piece of Mind. Close your eyes and let your imagination run wild with all the relaxing things you and Archangel Uriel can do together. Write out your creative angel ideas. Let this list build over time and bring more of the Heavenly Peaceful Frequencies into your life with Archangel Uriel.

9

JOURNALING WITH SAINT GERMAIN

Saint Germain wants to help you by offering his Ascended Master Consciousness. The book Vol 15 *Ascended Masters Speak on Angels* (Saint Germain Series) explains that as we visualize things, we are creating them. If we call on Saint Germain, he will help us hold our desired visions with more power more often for more pleasing manifestations. Journal all the beautiful mind pictures you would like to hold and bring about with Saint Germain's help.

10

FLOAT ON HEAVENLY CLOUDS WITH ARCHANGEL URIEL

Feel as Archangel Uriel lifts you with their magnificent wings and leads you to float with them on light, fluffy clouds. Let your imagination run wild, and journal all the fantastic places and things you see together. Feel as Archangel Uriel guides you to more angelic adventures of well-being and peace.

11

JOURNALING WITH ARCHANGEL URIEL FOR MORE MINDFULNESS

Relax as Archangel Uriel stands before you and Archangel Raziel behind you. Place your hand on your heart and enjoy as Archangel Uriel shimmers Angelic blue energy around you. Relax as Archangel Raziel brings brilliant saphire sprinkles of light, and the enlivening colors swirl around you as you feel calm and supported. Now take this Divine Peace feeling to your Journal pages.

12

BRING BLUE FLAME ANGELS IN TO PLAY WITH ARCHANGEL URIEL

Call the Blue Flame Angels to remove any nonbeneficial energies from your environment. Ask them to enlist their Angel Alchemy with Archangel Uriel to fill the spaces they create with Divine Peace and Freedom. Feel all these magnificent beings working on your behalf now. Feel your Power now and journal all about your experience. Imagine and feel all the blue angelic sparkles of light all around you. Be patient with yourself; you and your angels have this.

13
ALLOW ARCHANGEL URIEL TO INFUSE YOU WITH MORE PEACE

Archangel Raziel is your Archangel for Wisdom. Visualize Raziel infusing your Mind with Golden Shimmers of Wisdom. Now smile as Archangel Zadkiel joins the process to sprinkle Violet Sparkles through the golden to invigorate your knowledge. Journal all the fantastic wisdom ideas these magnificent Angels Inspire.

14

FEELING RADIANT WITH THE VIOLET FLAME

Please take a deep soothing breath and visualize as Archangel Zadkiel and Saint Germain stand with you and infuse you with their powerful Violet Flame frequencies. Feel the tingles and joy radiating—Journal how refreshing this energy feels. Find your Happy Place with the help of these Masters of Feeling Good Now.

MORE ANGEL IDEAS

15

CALL ARCHANGEL MICHAEL AND ARCHANGEL URIEL TO SECURE YOUR PEACE

Archangel Michael is your Archangel for Security. Visualize Archangel Michael using their Light Sword to cut any heavy cords away from you, helping you to feel lighter and brighter. Now smile as Archangel Uriel joins the process of sprinkling light blue sparkles through this angelic creation to invigorate your feeling of safety and peace. Journal all the fantastic, peaceful security feelings these magnificent Angels Inspire.

16

PROTECTIVE PEACE JOURNALING WITH SAINT MARTHA

Spend some time Journaling with Saint Martha. She is the Saint to call for Protection. Call her and Archangel Uriel to stand around you and protect your peace. Practice this as often as needed and journal your results and any ideas on other things you would like them to help you with. Faith is the art of seeing the unseen. Have faith that you have called the best and that things are working for you.

17

CALL ARCHANGEL URIEL FOR PEACEFUL GUIDANCE

Place reminders where you will see them often. Ask Archangel Uriel for guidance to more peace and journal what comes through. Visualize Archangel Uriel whispering great ideas in your ear. Imagine yourself smiling while this Divine Angel helps and supports you.

18

WALK IN PEACE WITH ARCHANGEL URIEL

Visualize as Archangel Uriel points to your feet, creating shimmering blue light circles around them. Feel the peace move from your feet up your body. See as the blue shimmering circles go everywhere your feet do in your imagination. Practice this Angel Magick anytime you want to feel and spread more Serenity. "Walk your talk" to more peaceful interactions in your life. Play with this regularly and write down all the benefits you experience. Be easy with this and enjoy the process.

19

ARCHANGEL URIEL AND THE ENLIGHTENED MASTER JESUS CHRIST

Visualize Archangel Uriel, the Princess/Prince of Peace, standing with you in solidarity for a peaceful world. Call this master of peaceful interactions, Archangel Uriel, to bring your world more Heaven on Earth. Feel as the Enlightened Master Jesus Christ stands before you, smiling and radiating peace. Relax as he points to your Heart Center, shimmering it with Divine Peace. Feel as Archangel Uriel joins this Divine Creation to stand behind you, shimmering Angelic Peace around you. Just breathe and feel as if you are in the center of the most peaceful place. Write out all the blessings that occur from this Divine vision. Practice anytime you need.

20

JOURNALING PEACE WITH ARCHANGEL URIEL

Allow any peaceful thoughts and feelings when you call Archangel Uriel to flow to your journal pages. Set intentions to spend time with Archangel Uriel and any of your other Archangels, writing all the peace you are calling into your life and your entire circle of influence. Bring your peaceful blessings to the people you love and your life.

21

CALLING IN PEACEFUL HEALTHY BOUNDARIES WITH ARCHANGEL URIEL

Call Archangel Uriel to stand around you with St. Martha. She is an expert at healthy boundaries. Ask these divine beings to help you have healthy boundaries filled with peace and support. Journal any areas of your life that you would like more healthy boundaries. Ask Archangel Uriel and St. Martha to dismantle any beliefs that you are not worthy of healthy boundaries and peace. Visualize these powerful beings creating all the healthy boundaries you desire.

22

FLOAT PEACEFULLY WITH ARCHANGEL URIEL

Relax as Archangel Uriel hugs you in their safe and supportive Angel Wings. Feel all the peace Archangel Uriel shimmers you with and all the blue flame Angels filling your field. Take Archangel Uriel's hand and do some Angel Floating through the clear, bright heavenly sky. Journal all the relaxation you are feeling and more.

23

PEACEFUL FREEDOM WITH ARCHANGEL URIEL AND ST. LUCY

St. Lucy is the Saint of seeing the unseen. Ask her to help Archangel Uriel show you more ways to see and feel peace in your world. When things feel out of order, call St. Lucy and Archangel Uriel to bring Peace and Protection to your life. Write in this Journal about how you would like to experience peace and Protection. Get creative and draw sacred geometry pictures of peace with the help of Archangel Metatron.

24

CALL FOR MORE PEACE IN YOUR ENVIORNMENT

Ask Archangel Uriel, with the help of Archangel Michael, to create 1 billion light doors in any space that needs more peace and security. Once you feel the light doors, ask Archangel Uriel and Archangel Michael to usher out any non-beneficial energies to the light or wherever they decide is best. Ask Archangel Haniel and Archangel Barachiel to fill any spaces created with Love, blessings, and, of course, Peace. You can do this in as little as 30 seconds once you practice. Do this as often as needed, and always do this before walking into a building. The Archangels have your back when you remember to call them. Get creative and write how to use this new skill in your Journal.

BLESSINGS

May the Divine Creative Force that Moves and Creates the Universes Bless and Enhance Every Wish You Ever Conceived that is for the Highest Good of All Involved. May Joy, Peace, and Purpose Be Yours all the Days of your Lives. Through All Time Space and Dimensions. So, Mote, it Be, and So It Is. I hope this book helps you in wonderful ways and radiates out to a gorgeous life for you and yours. May you always Be Blessed and Highly Favored.

Kim Caldwell, creator of the Archangelology Book and Audio Series

REFERENCES

Ascended Masters. Ascended Masters Speak on Angels (Saint Germain Foundation Printing.)

Diana Cooper. The Archangel Guide to Ascension: 55 Steps to Light. (Hay House Inc.)

Matias Flury. Downloads From The Nine: Awaken As You Read. (Matias Flury 2014).

MORE OFFERINGS

~

Visit https://archangelology.com to discover more Archangels and Super Power Saints

Each of the following books has a matching audio filled with healing music.

Archangelology Michael * Protection
Archangelology Raphael * Abundance
Archangelology Camael * Courage
Archangelology Gabriel * Hope
Archangelology Metatron * Well Being
Archangelology Uriel * Peace
Archangelology Haniel * Love
Archangelology Raziel * Wisdom
Archangelology Zadkiel * Forgiveness

Archangelology Jophiel * Glow

Archangelology Violet Flame * Oneness

Archangelology Sun Angels * Power

Archangelology Moon Angels * Magnetism

Archangelology Sandalphon * Harmony

Archangelology Orion * Expansion

The items below come in book only

Archangelology * Archangel Journaling

Archangelology * Archangel Breath-Tap Book

How Green Smoothies Saved My Life Book

Activate Your Abundance Book and Audio Program

The rest of the items below are available in Audio Format

Archangelology*Mary Magdalene*Feminine Divine Audio

Archangelology * Breath-Tap Super Power Saints Volume 1 Audio

Archangelology * Breath-Tap Super Power Saints Volume 2 Audio

Regeneration Meditations * Switchword Series with Solfeggio Frequencies audio

Radiating Divine Love * Switchword Series with Solfeggio Frequencies audio

Love Charm * Switchword Series with Solfeggio Frequencies audio

Dragon Sun Grounding Meditations * Cosmic Consciousness Series audios

Sweet Moon Sleep Meditation * Cosmic Consciousness Series

Enchanted Earth Sacred Geometry * Cosmic Consciousness Series audios

PLEASE WRITE A HELPFUL REVIEW

If you enjoyed this book please give a positive review so others may find it as well. And may blessings come back for your help.

Thank you so much. May you always be Blessed and highly favored.

Kim

www.ingramcontent.com/pod-product-compliance
Lightning Source LLC
Chambersburg PA
CBHW072010090426
42734CB00033B/2417